Stu

Stump Rope

BY

Steve Brhel

Cover Illustrated by:

Scott Matheson

Bookstand Publishing

www.bookstandpublishing.com

Published by
Bookstand Publishing
Morgan Hill, CA 95037
3669_3

Copyright © 2012 by Steve Brhel
All rights reserved. No part of this publication may be reproduced or transmitted in any form or by any means, electronic or mechanical, including photocopy, recording, or any information storage and retrieval system, without permission in writing from the copyright owner.

ISBN 978-1-61863-304-0

Printed in the United States of America

ACKNOWLEDGEMENTS

Someone once told me that a story is nothing more than putting your thoughts or ideas on paper in a manner so that a person can read and enjoy it.

It was the union of my parents that produced the genes which gave me the gift of writing. My parents also gave me the support and stability all through my creative years and into my adulthood making me the person I am today.

Starting in the sixth grade and even after graduating High School I always had teachers who encouraged me to write and develop my hidden talents. Some of them were difficult on me while others coaxed me in a more gingerly style. Either way, their results were all good.

In 1962 a dear friend, who fifty years later is still my best friend, encouraged me to pick a Jack London book on library day for our next book report in school. I remember not being able to put that book down because every page that I read was a vivid picture in my mind and I felt as if I was really there. I truly believe that is when I wanted to become a writer and someday have a story published.

The red tailed hawk glided to his perch in a favorite oak tree while firmly clutching his morning prey. His head dropped slowly watching the horseman below. Convinced that there was no threat, the bird began to consume an early breakfast high above the rider in his valley. The cowboy raised his head tipping a weathered hat to the majestic creature in a gesture of respect. There was a long day of work ahead for Tom Jackson and his horse Ginny, so the team kept moving. The hawk turned slightly to watch the pair amble across the pasture.

The morning was already turning warm as the sun began its daily ascent. Ginny kept her pace to a long walk as Tom Jackson observed a coyote on the hillside teaching her pup the survival art of catching a ground squirrel. The mother looked in Tom's direction for a moment only to disappear into the sagebrush with her young student. The animals truly lived up to their Native American name of 'ghosts' as they both vanished. Tom sat back in the saddle bringing Ginny to a stop and took in the panoramic scene through his office window. He thought to himself, 'great view from my desk…and the commute ain't half bad either'. He squeezed Ginny lightly with his legs and she resumed with her steady pace.

This was the only life that Tom Jackson had ever known or wanted. It was hard work but to him it was personally rewarding. He saw and experienced things that most people would only read about or could see in nature documentaries. He was simply a cowboy, a breed of man that was near being placed on the endangered species list. His friends jokingly referred to him in terms as relic, fossil, and dinosaur or when they really wanted to get his attention it was 'Hey, you old man …'

Tom Jackson was not a young kid by anybody's standards but he was not yet ready to be put out to pasture. There was still too much life left in this wrangler. He always joked that if he ever did sell the place and move to town that he would only be able to court the younger ladies. All of the women his own age were either buried or in the retirement home. Deep in his heart he knew he could never sell the ranch for any price. It was not because his grandfather's father had started this spread or that Tom could not adjust to city life, it was that little patch of land on the edge of the woods called Stump Rope. It was a place that Tom Jackson would visit when his memories would turn to loneliness. Everything he loved was there and he could never leave it behind.

The truck sped down the highway catching the morning sun on its windshield making it necessary for the driver to don his designer sunglasses. Peering past the lowered visor he had a better view of the bugs who decided to make the glass their final resting place. Thinking of what the other insect family members were doing to his polished chrome grill only added to his frustration and contempt for this whole area. Why did his cousin have to get married on this weekend and out in the middle of nowhere? Everyone thinks this is such a romantic way to have a wedding. He would rather be back at home knocking little white balls around the golf course with his buddies rather than wasting his free time like this. Every time something like this happens he swears it will be the last. He eased the cruise control up five miles per hour faster justifying the potential speeding ticket with the number of deceased insects that he was collecting at a much faster speed.

The young lady sat far to the passenger side of the speeding vehicle. She glanced to her left at the speedometer but kept her thoughts to herself, 'his truck, his gas pedal, his ticket'. If she did say anything it would just make him go even that much faster. Why do men act so mature when they are upset? It was at moments like this that she sometimes regretted not taking her parents up on those adolescent threats and going to live in the convent. A person does not have to be an Ophthalmologist to understand that hindsight is always 20/20. Meanwhile she would have to be content with refolding the map and trying to figure a good time to let him know that he should have taken Highway 29 South about ten miles back. He deserved a few more minutes of his 80-miles per hour maturity.

"Are you sure that you are reading the stupid map the right way?" Kevin finally asked keeping his stare fixed forward as two more Kamikaze grasshoppers hit their target and caused a vein to become visible in his neck.

"Yes, Kev honey," Shari answered with just enough verbal syrup on her drawl to cover the intended sarcasm. "I am sure that I am reading it just the way that you taught me. It is from the left to the right and from the top to the bottom and make certain that the pointy thing with the letter 'N' is always on top. Isn't that correct?"

Kevin finally glanced in her direction while he fumbled in the console for his ever trusty cell phone. If looks could truly kill a person perhaps Shari should now be thinking about the epitaph on her headstone. Perhaps something with a little humor, 'I told you that I was a bad cook'! Sometimes she felt like that phone was a life support machine for him and without it he could not function at any level in the real world. Deep down he actually was a fairly decent guy. He was like an artichoke you just had to peel enough layers away to find a heart. It could be worse than this, at least his parents had made him an only child.

"That pointy thing is called a compass and the 'N' means North and what is my cousin's phone number anyway?" He demanded while driving with one hand and attempting to dial the phone with the other. Shari just laid her head back and wondered about all the other men that she let get away. Speeding down the road at 85 miles per hour was probably not the best time to bring up 'sweetheart, we really do need to talk'!

Riding a fence line might be considered a bit dull for some folks but for Tom Jackson it was his thinking time. It always gave him a chance to just get lost in private thought and see where it would take him. He fortunately had his horse Ginny who would sometimes appear to have more smarts than him and today was no different than any other day. This horse had developed a habit for stopping whenever there was a break in the barbwire or there was a fence post on the ground. Today was no exception to the routine except that Tom Jackson was in deeper thought than usual and did not realize that Ginny had been standing patiently in the same spot for at least two minutes. Whenever this happened she always gave her body a good shake to get his attention and hear the usual reply.

"I know, I know, just thinking about something girl."

Tom gave Ginny's neck a hardy scratching with his right hand and leaned his left palm into the saddle horn while throwing his right leg behind him and dropped out of the saddle. When both of his feet were planted on the rocky ground he gave her some good pats on the rump and thanked her with a 'good girl'. She looked back over her left shoulder which was her horse talk for 'you are welcome, again'.

He walked to the fence post that was still attached to the barbwire and it was leaning just a few inches above the ground. The wire was stretched but unbroken. Tom removed his hat and slowly wiped his forehead with a clean bandana while reviewing the pending repair. He also took note of the warm sun nearly overhead which meant it was almost lunchtime. A minor half-hour repair on the fence and then he could have his midday meal. He walked back to Ginny and retrieved the necessary tools and thought about his talents as a 'bovine enclosure engineer'. Even an old cowboy must be politically correct in this modern world when it came to doing a repair on his cattle fence. This thinking kept a grin and whistle on his lips during the next forty minutes of fence fixing.

Kevin and Shari had been together for nearly a year. Just like most couples they had their good and bad times. Keeping the balance on the love scale lately seemed like a full time job for Shari. Kevin was always so wrapped up in his work that he was on edge about everything. At a young age he was financially successful but the more money he earned the less time he had for Shari. He was able to give her anything she wanted and he did just that. What she wanted more than anything was the romance of the early days when there were more hugs and his words 'I love you'.

"Did you find my cousin's phone number yet?" He asked sternly.

"Yes. Just give me your phone and I will dial it for you. It would be a shame if you were to miss any of these bugs," she calmly replied.

Kevin passed the phone to her and waited an eternity while she punched in the numbers by memory. Ever so slowly she handed the phone back to him making sure that he had it firmly in his hand. He quickly brought it to his ear.

The conversation with his cousin was quite brief and to the point. It seems that they had missed the turnoff just a few miles back in the other direction. This was simple enough. This was just the perfect touch to an already perfect day on the most perfect weekend of his entire life.

"Why didn't you tell me to take Highway 29 South?" He yelled as he threw the cell phone on the seat.

"I do believe that was about the time you felt quite confident that you knew your way around here and even made a point to tell me that fact in those exact words Kevin," Shari shot back raising her voice.

"You are too much, you know that!" Kevin bellowed.

"There is only one thing I know right now and that is for you to calm down and do not even raise your voice at me Kevin R. Daley!" She shouted.

Shari's firm disposition took Kevin completely by surprise. It was probably not the most opportune time for him to attempt getting in the last word. It was not that he didn't savor the victory but diplomacy seemed the best route to take at the moment. The return trip to Highway 29 South felt like the longest and most quiet ten miles ever endured by a young couple so much in love. The only sound to be heard was the light blowing of the air conditioner, which added to an already existing chill in the cab of the truck.

Tom Jackson had always taken pride in anything he did, even a minor fence repair as this. He quickly gathered his tools and took a few seconds to stand and admire his handy-work. He thought back to his youth and his own father teaching Tom and his older brother the value in knowing how to work with your own two hands. It all seemed such a long time ago.

As he walked back to Ginny with the tools he realized just how hungry he was and that is when the shock hit him. He felt anger, famish and plain stupid all in one. The lunch that he could not wait to devour was still sitting on his kitchen table. He remembered putting it on the table to answer the phone when he was heading out the door and now, due to an early morning wrong number, he had no lunch.

"Well, Ginny, it appears we are both in a bit of a bind girl." He stated as he put the tools back into the saddlebag.

"I have no lunch, which means you and I are going to take a little trip into town. We can use the exercise. You do the running and I will do the riding. Same as always girl," he chuckled as he rubbed her behind the ear.

Fortunately, they were at the North end of his ranch, which put them about three miles from town. It would be faster to go into town and eat than to ride all the way back to the house. As he climbed back into the saddle he squeezed Ginny into a walk down the hill. Sitting back with his boots forward in the stirrups he gave the horse her head. The hill was steep so he let Ginny choose the safest path to the grassy meadow below. When they reached the valley bottom Tom walked Ginny for almost ten minutes and then eased her into a smooth lope for another quarter mile. Extending both the reins Tom touched the base of her neck and gently put his boot heels to her side and said,

"Let's stretch you out girl." The horse and rider now became one at a gallop.

There is nothing more exciting than watching nature fly by you while on the back of a smart horse at a full run. This thrill never lessened for Tom Jackson. He would keep her at this speed for about another two miles and then give the horse a much deserved break at Stump Rope. Tom could cool her down by the creek and it would give him some time to think about his wife and son. It had been a while since he spent any time with his family at Stump Rope.

The red 4x4 pickup truck slowed its speed as it made a smooth left merge onto the southbound highway. The two lane road stretched far ahead becoming a thin line that eventually just disappeared. The occupants of the vehicle both knew that the silence could not last forever but for now the mile markers and continual parade of windshield bugs would be their only solace. Each person would wait in silence allowing the other the opportunity to make the first apology. The only problem on this lonely highway was that neither person was at fault because they both felt that the other one started it.

This was a simple case of two grown adults acting like children on their way to a family wedding in the middle of nowhere. This would be a minimum two page entry into her diary tonight. He watched the clock on the radio knowing that he needed to make an important business call but felt it was not the best ice breaker to use at the moment. Kevin and Shari kept their thoughts to themselves while pretending to enjoy the asphalt bliss.

A half mile out Tom reined Ginny back and sat a little deeper in the saddle to bring her to a lope and then into a nice steady walk. This allowed her a chance to start cooling down as she long-stepped the remainder of the way to Stump Rope. This area had always had such a calm and spiritual feeling that a person could not explain but just had to feel the experience.

This is the spot where Tom Jackson courted Kelley O'Brien for what seemed like an eternity of trail rides and picnics until he finally found the courage to ask her to be his wife. He remembered how direct her answer was to him.

"Why did you wait so long to ask me, Tom Jackson? You have only been in love with me since the tenth grade!"

The picnics continued long after Tom Junior was born. No matter how much his mother fought it, this little boy was a natural cowboy from the moment he took his first steps. He was fearless, loved horses in all sizes and colors and had a natural balance in the saddle.

When Tom Junior was three years old he started throwing a rope and with some good accuracy. There was an old stump that he would practice on with his lasso while his parents sat nearby on the picnic blanket. Tom Jackson promised his son that when he was five years old he could go along to help bring in the wild horses that still roamed the upper valleys. Finally the day came when Tom Junior told his daddy that he was too old to keep using 'Stump Rope' and that he was ready to go out with the crew and earn his keep. The maternal protests gave way to the fact that Kelley Jackson had given birth to a die-hard cowboy who stood a tall five years old.

That same afternoon the mother and son drove into town to buy the supplies for his first roundup that would last no more than three days. The crew would get an early start the next morning and with some luck Tom Junior would have a horse of his own. That was nearly twenty-seven years ago and whenever Tom Jackson visited Stump Rope, it always seemed like it just happened yesterday.

Tom quickly turned and knelt down at the creek to wash his face in the cool water and then dry his eyes. Ginny walked over to him and nudged him with her nose letting him know she was ready to go. It was an easy half-mile trot to the edge of the ranch at Highway 29 where they could cross at the curve and then go to Harley's.

"Ginny, I do hope you don't mind if we stop at Harley's Diner," Tom said. "You can rest out back with a little feed while I am inside eating and having a visit with my old buddy."

Her whinny was the only approval Tom Jackson needed to hear. Horses have their rights also in this part of the country and Ginny was no exception to the rule. The team headed North with the sun now over their left shoulders.

"Shari," Kevin said softly still looking straight ahead. "I know I can be a real idiot at times and this is definitely one of those times. I am really sorry for losing my temper with you."

Shari sat there in calm thought and mentally digested what Kevin had just said. He reminded her of a little boy bringing home a note from school for getting into trouble on the playground.

"Kevin, you know it seems like this is happening more and more these days and it is becoming a regular part of you," she responded keeping her voice steady. "I know that you have an awful lot on your mind with work but I am not going to let you use that as your defense anymore!" She firmly stated.

He knew she was right as always and he also knew that he was a lucky man to not only have such a wonderfully beautiful lady but that she also put up with his attitudes. He did not want to lose her. It was difficult for him but at this moment what he really needed was some basic personal humility.

"Honey, what can I do to make it better for you?" He asked with a begging tone in his voice.

"First of all, it is not what you can do for me, it is for us Kevin. We are a couple, a team who works together towards being happy no matter what is thrown at us," she responded without making it sound like she was on her soap box. "I simply want you to spend a little more time with me and do it because you want to do it and not that you have to do it. I know that your job is very important but I think that I am also just as important. Don't you agree?" She queried.

"Yes, you are right. You are the most important person in my life and I do not want to lose you, ever. Will you work with me on this if I promise to change?" He asked.

"Sweetheart, I am not trying to change you. I just want you to take a close look at how you treat me and everybody else in this big world. Just take the time to enjoy life when you can," she answered.

"First thing we do, Kevin, is stop at the next restaurant so you can feed me because I am starving. I know that you need to make that phone call that you mentioned this morning and also you must buy a big tube of lip balm," she declared in a matter of fact way.

"Why a big tube of lip balm?" He questioned with a puzzled look on his face.

"Kevin, I am a reasonable lady but at the same time practical," she mused. "Starting today, Sir, you have a good month of butt kissing to do on this girl!"

This gave them both a good laugh and it lightened the mood for the next few miles as they neared the little town that advertised 'Harley's Diner ... Good Eats'. Everything was going well until Kevin came around the curve a little too fast to safely negotiate a broken exhaust pipe lying in their lane. Kevin's attempt to miss the rusty piece of metal made him over-steer the truck and slide into the wide shoulder. This gave him the opportunity to hold the truck on a straight path angled back towards the road. The panic was mild even with the dust and gravel flying but everything seemed under control, except for the horse and cowboy who were trying to decide on their next move.

"Kevin, do you see that rider?" Shari screamed with terror in her voice.

Tom Jackson put his left hand and reins under the front of the saddle and stepped into the stirrup as he swung his right leg over Ginny in one easy motion. He gave her the rein to walk and then step into a good trot. Ten minutes later the rider and horse were at the edge of the fence line which was at the most northern section of Tom Jackson's ranch and on the other side was Highway 29 South. Tom quickly dismounted and opened the barbwire gate allowing enough room to walk Ginny through it. Once she was clear of it he re-strung the gate.

Ginny proceeded up the embankment with Tom securely in the saddle and both readied to cross the highway. It was only a two lane road which did not see much traffic these days but you always wanted to keep an eye on the curve to the left side. There was always going to be that one driver who would attempt taking it much faster than common sense would allow.

Tom and Ginny looked up and down the road in both directions and it appeared clear to cross. As Tom gently coaxed Ginny with his heels and made a couple of clicking sounds with his mouth she took two steps forward and stopped just short of the asphalt. Tom softly tried to push her forward but she wanted nothing to do with this maneuver. Ginny became instantly alert with both ears forward and moving them from left to right and quickly back to the left. She suddenly retreated four steps and it was at that moment that Tom saw the red 4x4 pickup truck sliding through the gravel and heading straight for the horse and rider. What happened next was simply a cowboy trusting the logic of a very wise horse. Ginny threw her head back and brought both front legs three feet off the ground which let her sit on her haunches. This gave her enough momentum to spin a half-circle and jump ten feet in the direction they had just ridden. The pickup truck roared by them with less than a yardstick for clearance.

Tom realized his left hand was still gripped around the saddle horn as the dust settled and his heart returned to a normal pace. All things considered, Ginny was back to being herself other than her nostrils appearing a bit larger than normal. Tom carefully got off Ginny lowering the reins over her head and stood directly in front of her. He quietly rubbed her cheeks and placed a long kiss on her muzzle while she patiently endured his affections. The cowboy and his horse shared the silence for a few more moments.

Tom led Ginny to the edge of the road and watched the truck still speeding down the highway probably on its way to town. The driver looked straight ahead while the female passenger watched out the rear window until she saw the horse and rider appear at the roadside. She slowly turned towards the driver and firmly pushed his head with her hand while giving him some type of verbal guidance. Tom felt a little relief knowing that they were all right too. He turned his attention back to Ginny.

"Girl, I promised you a trip to town and you know that I always live up to my word," he calmly whispered to her. "I will leave it up to you."

Ginny put her forehead on Tom's chest and then looked up at him while bouncing her head up and down. Tom climbed back into the saddle and rubbed the right side of her neck. She let out a long whinny and snorted.

"Kinda' thought that is how you'd feel, so now let's go see Harley!" He laughed.

The remainder of the ride to town felt rather dull after what had just happened to Tom and Ginny. Tom Jackson tried to shake it off but he could not let it go. This stretch of highway had a dangerous and even deadly history and it made Tom's memory drift back many years ago to an accident that had taken place in almost the same area as today. Tom Jackson's life was changed forever in an instant on that day. He eventually worked through it but never completely understood why a tragedy like that has to occur in a good person's life. He stretched forward in the saddle with a long left arm and gave Ginny a good hard tickle between the ears as she brought her head up to meet the motion of his hand. This horse had more than earned her keep today and Tom was grateful.

Some things just never change in life and Harley's Diner was at the top of the page in this category. Harley White was a 'to-it' type of man. He always had things he needed to 'get to' but just never quite found the time to accomplish these tasks. 'I will get to-it as soon as I have the time' was his trademark saying. The first time Tom had ever heard him use this expression was back in the fifth grade when Harley did not have his book report assignment ready for their teacher, Mrs. Duncan. She was so impressed with his logic that she let Harley stay after school and write this now famous quote on the blackboard one hundred times. It was probably then that Harley White decided this was the path that he would follow throughout his lifetime, 'I will get to-it as soon as I have the time'.

Tom dropped the bit from Ginny's mouth and wrapped the lead rope around the hitching rail with years of personalized initial carvings, bite marks and still in need of a new nail to secure it to one of the posts. After hanging the bridle on his saddle horn he then gave the rail a shove with his right hand and felt it would last for another year on Harley's repair list. He walked up to the barrel at the base of the steps and scooped a can of oats which he brought back to the bucket tied to the railing in front of Ginny. He reached to the right in order to feel the water in the trough and at the same time he gave her forehead a touch with his free hand. She was already enjoying a well-earned lunch as Tom walked back to the top of the porch and tossed the can down into the feed barrel. He looked at Ginny there by herself and thought about the days when a dozen horses would have been standing with her. It just proves that cowboys became a little softer when Detroit City began installing air conditioning into their pickup trucks. Tom turned to the back door, kicked the dust off his boots and walked into a busy day at Harley's Diner.

"No ma'am, I am quite sure that I do not use any M-S-G in my burgers. If an ingredient has to be spelled then it does not go into any of my food. The reason I only serve that box wine, as you so call it, is because it stacks quite neatly in the trunk of my car when I make the weekly supply run to the grocery depot over in Fairville," Harley politely convinced the lady.

Harley White took in a large breath of air while at the same time raised one eyebrow and slowly set the huge hamburger and glass of wine in front of the customer. She continued to stare at the meal in front of her as Harley turned and walked back to the cash register.

"I see that you still need to put a nail in that hitching rail out back," Tom taunted Harley when he turned back to face the bar.

"I am going to get to it as soon as I can find the time old man, but I don't really see the need to rush since you are about the only cowboy left around here that still uses it!" Harley shot back with a grin. "How are you and Ginny doing these days?" He asked his friend.

The two men, who were still best of friends since the infamous book report incident in Mrs. Duncan's class, stuck out their right hands and joined them in a firm handshake. This was a friendship that had weathered much throughout both of their lives and each man knew that he would always be there for the other one regardless of the reason. They both had shared events in their lives that were good, some were bad and those that you just left alone.

"Tom, can you do me a favor and walk out front and see if there is a big tour bus sitting in my parking lot?" Harley pleaded.

"Sure, but can I ask why?" Tom inquired.

"I just have a hunch that the 'Big Dumb Ass' Convention is in town again and they all came here for lunch! Please just humor your friend and go take a look for me," he begged.

Tom Jackson knew the routine so he walked out to the front porch and scanned the parking lot for the imaginary bus. As usual, there was not a bus to be seen anywhere but what did catch Tom's eye was a red 4x4 pickup truck parked off to the far side of the lot. Perhaps now would be a good time for Tom to dispense some neighborly advice combined with his fatherly compassion. He returned to the counter to hear Harley concluding a discussion with another customer regarding the need for balsamic vinegars in his eating establishment. Harley White still had both hands on the edge of the bar and was shaking his head as Tom approached him.

"There was no sign of that bus you three legged horse trader," Tom reported. He sat down to a barbecued chicken sandwich and an iced tea that Harley had waiting for him.

"Did you happen to notice the couple who is driving that red 4x4 out there?" He asked looking Harley in the eye with a sense of seriousness.

"Yeah, I did as a matter of fact. They are at the fourth table by the window. She is the pretty brunette and he is the one with that cell phone stuck to his ear. She has had a peculiar look on her face since they walked in here. She ate her lunch really fast and has been waiting for him to get off of the phone this whole time. I think he is using it as a stall technique myself," Harley summarized.

"Tom, how did we ever communicate before we had all of these electronic gadgets in our lives?" Harley questioned.

"It was much simpler back then Harley. If a person had a true emergency you would use your party line. If someone else was on it, you politely broke in and told them the situation. The people who did not have that luxury would saddle up their fastest horse and ride to the nearest neighbor who had a phone. If it was a non-emergency then you waited for the monthly meeting at the Grange Hall and that is where you would catch up on all of the news and gossip." Tom concluded his oratory on the easier way of life.

"Why are you so interested in that particular couple Tom?" Harley pressed him for more information.

"Well, let's just say we met due to a lack of his driving skills and etiquette back at the curve where I cross the highway. If it had not been for that horse I have tied out back you would be inheriting my ranch about now," Tom stated.

Tom Jackson thanked his friend for the lunch and tried to pay him but Harley White would hear of no such thing in his diner. Tom spun the barstool, stood up and pulled the hat firmly on his head. He walked in the direction of the fourth table by the window.

Shari pushed the dirty plate to the edge of the table as the waitress reached to add it to the collection already cradled in her right arm. Looking at the barely touched food in front of Kevin the lady glanced at Shari for an approval on this call. The simple side-to-side movement of Shari's head meant for the waitress to leave it because now he deserved the lukewarm food. She nodded at Shari with a smile and moved on to the next table. The waitress just hoped that the fireworks would take place out in the parking lot and not inside the diner.

"What do you mean that they want to think about it?" Kevin barked into the phone. "You were supposed to close this deal today so we could start on it Monday. Am I supposed to do your job for you? Here is how you handle these jerks ....!"

As he verbally listed the instructions, Kevin gave Shari the signal that he would only be on the phone for a few more minutes. She looked straight through him wondering what his blood pressure read at times like this. If it became too high would his body really take on the form of a thermometer with the mercury rising so fast that it could cause his head to explode just like in the cartoons? Today just might be the day to test this comical theory.

Shari turned her attention back to people watching and trying to guess everyone's occupation. She mentally noted the struggling actress, a tennis pro, he had to be a doctor, she was a lawyer, that man definitely drives a big rig and then she noticed the man in the old hat slowly making his way through the tables and customers. Now this man was a real cowboy if ever in her life she had seen one. He had a gentle look for an older man and he was still quite handsome. Shari could hear her grandmother telling her with the incorrect grammar necessary to make her point,

"Now, that is one wrangler that scrubs up pretty good girl!"

Shari turned her attention to the parking lot and the scenery beyond the cars and trucks. This part of the country was even more beautiful than the rest of the state and she thought how easily she could live here. It reminded her of her younger days when she would stay with her grandparents for the summers and how welcome they always made her feel during those visits. She made a mental note that she would call them when she returned home from this trip.

Shari suddenly snapped back to the present when she felt someone standing next to her. She looked up to see the cowboy at their table. It was then that she realized that he was the same man on horseback whom Kevin had nearly killed back on the highway. The kindness in Tom Jackson's eyes put her at ease.

"Good afternoon ma'am, my name is Tom Jackson," he politely introduced himself to Shari.

At the same time he removed his hat and put out his right hand to shake her hand. Shari automatically extended her arm out while staying seated. She remembered her grandpa always telling her how to tell a real cowboy from a 'dresser up'. The real cowboy takes his hat off to a lady.

"How do you do?" She answered back. "I am Shari Lynne Marie," she stated while giving his hand a good squeeze.

Tom made a two-part approval noise from his throat.

"Mmm ... hhh, a young lady with three first names and a solid handshake. Kinda' rare these days."

"This is my boyfriend Kevin," she said turning her head in his direction.

Kevin looked at Tom Jackson while bringing his right hand up slowly. Tom began to push his hand in Kevin's direction only to find he was grabbing for empty air. Kevin had brought his hand up to his head for the simple purpose of plugging his free ear with his index finger enabling him to hear his phone better. At the same time Kevin turned his left shoulder allowing Tom a good view of his back. Tom tried to recover by wiping some imaginary dust from his jeans. He looked back at Shari to find her chin resting on her two hands almost as if she was in meditation. She slowly opened her eyes.

"You will have to excuse my boyfriend, Mr. Jackson," she apologized with enough volume so that both men could hear her.

"Kevin works very hard all week at being an idiot. He just does not realize that today is his day off!" She slowly shook her head and let out a sigh loud enough for the tennis pro and two girls at the next table to hear her.

"That's quite okay young lady, everybody deserves a day off every now and then," Tom chuckled back at her. "The reason I came over here was to see if you two are all right after that informal introduction we had back there on the highway, and please, call me Tom, Mr. Jackson was my father."

"Mr. Jack ... Tom! I am so sorry for what happened out there," Shari blurted. "There was something in the road and Mr. Manners next to me here tried to avoid it. He was going too fast and that put us into the gravel. The next thing you and your horse were right there and did we hurt either of you?" Shari gasped.

"First of all ma'am, you need to come up for some air and secondly, yes, Ginny and I came through it without a scratch. We are both doing just fine. Probably the only thought on my horse's mind right now is how to get up to the big barrel so that she can get some more oats," he explained with a soothing voice.

Shari stood up from the table and looked Tom Jackson straight in the eyes. It was her turn to put out a hand to him.

"Tom, thank you ... thank you very much. You are a true gentleman and they are kinda' rare these days. It is truly an honor to meet a man like you."

As they shook hands Shari could feel his genuine warmth. This man had a true sense of honesty.

"Now you two kids have a safe trip and you make sure that Kevin enjoys his day off," Tom teased her. "If you are ever this way again, please do not hesitate to stop by for a visit. I am in the book." Tom Jackson turned and began heading back towards the bar.

Kevin had finally finished his all-important call. Placing the cell phone on the table he turned towards Shari and questioned her with a bit of sarcasm in his voice.

"So, what did the hick want?"

He knew instantly that he had just said the worst thing to the wrong lady.

"Kevin R. Daley, you are the r-u-d-e-s-t man in the whole wide world!!!" She screamed and made sure to articulate every single word.

Kevin felt every customer looking at their table. He thought about quickly gazing through the window towards the parking lot but he was sure that the folks out there had also heard Shari. The waitress now in the kitchen just nodded her head towards the dishwasher and handed over her lost wager. She grumbled something under her breath about a sucker bet.

It was not the volume of Shari's voice that stopped Tom Jackson dead in his tracks, but it was that name, Kevin R. Daley. A cold chill ran all the way through his body and it seemed to just stick in his chest. He turned slowly and walked back to the fourth table by the window that was now the afternoon floorshow at Harley's Diner. He stood there for the longest time trying to get the question out that only the blushing young man could answer.

"Is your mother Angela Daley?" Tom Jackson asked coldly.

"She goes by Angie, but how would you know that?" Kevin shot back.

"Is her maiden name Schillert?" Tom asked again.

Kevin nodded a simple yes while Shari watched the gentleman cowboy. She now saw a look of pain in his kind eyes as he said a simple thank you and walked back to the bar. He sat down in front of the man everyone called Harley.

"Tom, you look like you have just seen a ghost. The last time I saw that look was right after the ...!" Harley stopped abruptly realizing what he had almost said.

"Harley, do you still keep that bottle under the bar? The one that you took from me many years ago just for safe keeping?" Tom inquired looking straight ahead.

"Well, if you are thinking about a drink then I will have to charge you extra. The big city bars would call it aged liquor," Harley laughed attempting to lighten the moment.

"No, I do not want a drink. I just wanted to make sure you had not drunk my bottle on me," Tom confessed. "What I could use is a good friend to go out on the back porch and give me some moral support. I think they call that male bonding these days."

Harley White felt the urgency in his friend's voice. As the two walked through the back door Harley tossed his soiled apron on the stack of beer cases while keeping his free hand on Tom's shoulder.

The young couple sat at the fourth table by the window in silence and were oblivious to the stares and whispers from the other tables. No one was quite sure what had just happened during the trio's brief encounter, but one thing was apparent to the locals and the visitors in Harley's Diner and that something had shaken the cowboy in the old hat.

Kevin and Shari quietly got up from the table and made their way to the cashier by the door. Kevin paid the bill and muttered something about keeping the change as he returned the money clip to his front pocket. They turned and walked towards the door not even hearing the lady thank Kevin for his generous gratuity that would more than cover her earlier financial loss to the dishwasher.

There were still eyes watching them and fingers being pointed in their direction from inside Harley's Diner as they walked across the dirt parking lot. The theories and assumptions were already being formulated by the lunch crowd experts as to what had really just happened. The tennis pro jokingly told the two girls that he would watch it all on the 11:00 o'clock news tonight.

Kevin was silent as he opened the door for Shari and then walked to his side of the truck and climbed in behind the steering wheel. As he attempted to slide the key into the ignition, Kevin realized that his hand was shaking slightly and enough for Shari to notice. She decided to remain quiet about it and not quite sure why. Kevin let the engine idle a few moments before he slipped the gearshift into the drive position. As soon as Kevin was confident that it was clear, he drove through the maze of vehicles and made his way to the exit sign at the end of the driveway. The truck proceeded to turn right and take the two occupants North onto Highway 29. His cousin's wedding did not seem all that important now. Anyway, this matrimonial venture made number three for him and Kevin was certain that his cousin would understand that they would attend his next wedding.

Tom Jackson was pacing back and forth while Harley White sat on the dilapidated bench with a broken armrest. This was another one of Harley's projects on his mental fix-it list. It was probably a good idea to let Tom keep moving since there was actually not enough room for both men to fit in this soon-to-be antique piece of furniture. Even with Tom's slim build, Harley's true love of late night desserts and cold beer would not allow such a seating venture to take place. It would be best to keep his friend on his feet and in a vertical motion. Harley was only thinking about maintaining Tom's good health as he finished the half-full bottle of beer in one swallow. He gently placed the empty bottle between his feet while taking some personal pride in the fact that the glass was still cold.

"Are you absolutely sure about this?" Harley asked breaking the stillness.

"Harley, I will bet the ranch on it. It must be him. I am certain!" Tom responded.

Harley removed his Yankees baseball cap and pushed his stubby fingers through the thick white hair. He knew Tom was right but was not sure in what direction to take this conversation. He would do anything for his friend but at the same time he did not want to bring back the memories from nearly thirty years ago.

"Even if you are right Tom, it ain't gonna' change the past. Please, for me just let it go," Harley appealed with compassion in his voice.

"Yeah, you were never the smartest kid in school and I was directly behind you in that line but you have always had just good common sense about life. This seems to be another one of those times. Thank you Harley," Tom said while shaking his friend's hand.

Harley carefully pushed himself out of the seat and at the same time hoping that the loose arm would support his weight. He wrapped his burly arms around Tom and gave him a solid hug as Tom tried to return the act of friendship in the best manner that was possible.

"Damn Harley, I cannot even get my hands to touch behind you!" Tom howled.

"Well, it ain't like we're dancing at the church social you old man!" Harley shot back.

The two friends pushed each other away still laughing at each other. Harley was relieved to see that Tom was back to being himself and Tom was happy at just having Harley there. The two men walked over to Ginny who was still waiting patiently. She swished her tail at a fly that had become both a pest and a companion during her stay. Just like Tom, she was ready to head for home. Tom slipped the bit into Ginny's mouth and adjusted her bridle. He then secured the lead rope around the horn and climbed back into the saddle. He said goodbye to Harley and gently turned Ginny in the direction that they both knew too well. It had been a long day for both of them.

There was a little more traffic on the highway than earlier that day. Kevin tilted his head forward just enough to swing the sun visor over the driver's door to block the glare of the warm mid-day sun. His windshield now had the resemblance of an entomologist's lecture board on the indigenous varieties of insects native to this part of the world. The dirty glass kept his mind occupied and let him avoid the inevitable conversation with the lady with the three first names sitting on the other side of his truck. Kevin drew a big breath and pushed the words out ever so slowly.

"Shari, please do not be mad at me," Kevin ventured with some hesitation.

Shari Lynne Marie sat quietly with her hands folded on her lap. She was still thinking about the diner and the look in Tom Jackson's eyes when he returned to their table. She could not explain it but it was a combination of fear, pain, rage, and almost as if he had just been awakened from a frightening nightmare. It was the type that would take a person a few minutes to realize that it was all a bad dream. Shari could not shake the image in her mind of Tom Jackson's face.

"Shari, are you going to talk to me?" Kevin pleaded.

"Kevin R. Daley, do not push your thin luck. I can be mad at you later but I am more concerned right now with what happened back at the diner. Didn't you see the expression on that man's face? It is very obvious that he somehow knew your mother!" She challenged.

"Even if he had known my mother, why would that upset the guy?" Kevin asked.

"Kevin, it was not that he knew your mother," Shari continued, "but it was your name that stopped him in his tracks. He went from being a very nice man to almost a scared child."

The next question that Shari was about to ask Kevin was very difficult for her. Even as upset as she was with Kevin she knew that any discussion of his father was a subject that few people wanted to mention, especially Kevin. Shari was very careful about the next words out of her own mouth.

"Wasn't your father's name, Kevin R. Daley?" Shari held her breath.

"I do not have a father!" He shot back coldly.

"Kevin, I do not mean to hurt you but just stop and think about it. Wouldn't that make them about the same age if your father were still alive? You have always told me that your mother was originally from this area and that you were born somewhere around here. It does make sense if you do the math." Shari theorized.

Kevin remained quiet as he gripped the steering wheel and thought about what Shari was saying. He knew without a doubt that she was correct. Somehow, a father whom he had never known was responsible for whatever had just taken place back at Harley's. A man who was not even a memory in Kevin's life could still find ways to keep hurting the son he left behind. The hate for this man was the only feeling that Kevin ever had for him. He sometimes wondered what he would have said to this man if he had ever had the opportunity. Kevin realized Shari's hand was on his shoulder as she leaned over to kiss his wet cheek. Her touch eased the tension and helped Kevin relax his thoughts.

Suddenly Kevin caught the movement on the highway as a pair of coyotes ran at full speed attempting to cross the asphalt. They were so close to each other that the smaller one of the two seemed as if it was attached to the larger animal's tail. Shari's scream instinctively made Kevin jerk at the steering wheel trying to avoid hitting the predators. The fast action saved their lives but it sent the truck skidding across the road and slicing cleanly through a barbwire fence. Kevin had both feet buried into the brake pedal as he held the steering wheel as straight as humanly possible for the longest and most frightening three hundred feet of their lives. It finally came to an end as the dust settled and the red 4x4 pickup truck was perched on the top of a large dirt mound in the middle of a pasture decorated with the droppings of its inhabitant bovines.

The Sheriff of the small town had also put in a long day. He had been on the trail of a bad man who needed to be apprehended at any price. This man was considered armed and dangerous and was a threat to anyone who got in his way. He had used his gun earlier and had taken the life of an innocent citizen. The Sheriff was taking this personal. The victim had been his own brother.

The young lawman could wait no longer for his backup to arrive and he knew the chance that he was taking as he cautiously peered around the edge of the alley. He was able to see the killer sitting behind the trash dumpster as he counted the stolen money. A chrome pistol rested on his lap as the late afternoon sun reflected off the polished metal. The Sheriff felt his own heart pumping all the way to the temples in his head. He silently tried to swallow the knot in his throat. His hand drew the revolver from its leather holster as he stepped from his hiding place.

"Police ... don't move!" He hollered. "Put those hands up!"

The killer was caught off guard by the Sheriff's command. The only movement was as his head slowly turned to the end of the alley. He held the currency tightly in his dirty hands as he fixed his eyes on the gun pointed directly at his heart. The light breeze caught the bills as he relaxed his fingers and reached for his own weapon. No other words were spoken as the sheriff carefully squeezed the trigger and repeated the action two more times. He stayed in place as the smoke drifted upwards from the barrel. He kept it trained on the lifeless body as he walked over and kicked the pistol a few feet away. It did not have to end like this.

Tom Jackson sat quietly in his saddle. Ginny's ears were still pointed in the direction of the gunshots. She watched the young man holster his gun and walk back towards her. She shifted her weight when he stopped next to her and looked up at the man on her back. Tom leaned over, put out his hand and pulled the Sheriff up all in one smooth motion. He sat him in front of the saddle and looked him straight in the eyes.

"That was some pretty fancy shootin' Jimmy," Tom exclaimed.

"Thanks Mr. Jackson," Jimmy answered with a toothless grin. "I had no choice. You know he was going for his gun."

"I know, I witnessed the whole thing," Tom attested to the seven-year-old as he tickled him in the ribs.

Jimmy squealed with enjoyment as his older brother walked over to join them, knocking the alley dirt off his shirt before stuffing the colored monopoly money into the top pocket. Shading his eyes, David greeted Tom with a question.

"What brings you to town Mr. Jackson?" David asked politely.

"Well boys, Ginny and I had some business with Harley White that could not wait any longer," Tom answered with a serious tone.

"You forgot your lunch again, didn't you Mr. Jackson?" Jimmy giggled still grinning.

"You got me Sheriff! That is what really happened, but I was able to have a nice visit with my old friend Harley," Tom responded.

He also thought how difficult it was becoming to put anything over on these boys. It made him think of himself and his own brother at about their same ages. The fun they had playing similar games as both Jimmy and David Bowlen did. That was many years ago.

Tom gently picked up Jimmy and softly dropped him to the ground with the assistance of his older brother.

"Now, if you two are free next Saturday, ask your parents to bring you out to the ranch. It has been a spell since the Bowlen family has been there for a visit," Tom encouraged.

"Can we all go to Stump Rope Mr. Jackson?" Both brothers fired excitedly back at Tom.

"Only if your momma brings one of her apple pies for the picnic," Tom replied already savoring the thought of such a treat.

"You have your mother call me this week, okay? Now be sure to clean and reload those cap guns," he instructed them over his right shoulder as he started to walk Ginny in the direction of the highway.

"That is a promise, Mr. Jackson!" David shouted as they both waived goodbye to Tom and Ginny. "I will make sure she calls you!"

"Ginny, what do you say we take the other way home so that you can do some more running?" Tom asked her. "You need to work off those oats you had at Harley's today!"

She quickly brought her head back and threw it from side to side making Tom take up the slack in the reins. She then high stepped and let out a snort from deep in her chest.

"That is what I thought also girl. Let's get going!"

The evening breeze pushed the blades of grass as the horse and rider galloped against the endless motion of green waves. It was difficult to determine who was enjoying it more, Tom Jackson or his horse Ginny. The equation was simple, she loved to run and he knew how to ride. They shared the feeling of youth and it made them both happy.

After nearly two miles, Tom began to slow Ginny and bring her to a trot. As they topped the knoll, Tom and Ginny were greeted with a strong gust of wind and a strange sight in the pasture below them. He pulled the horse to a sudden stop and quickly stood up in the saddle for a better view. Tom moved his head from side to side in utter disbelief.

"Ginny, today is just not our day!" He moaned. "Let's go down and see if they can use our help girl."

Nearly a half-mile away sat a red 4x4 pickup truck in a precarious position even for a vehicle of its magnitude. The bump in the ground, which was now its resting place, was not that large but this particular spot of earth made it impossible for any one of its four wheels to get traction. It had all of the appearance of a boat just sitting calmly in a dry dock.

The dark haired young lady patiently sat on a suitcase about twenty yards from the stranded vehicle with her long legs stretched out in front of her. She was propped up on her elbows with her head tilted back and eyes closed. She was enjoying the warm sunshine on her face and thinking that even this was somehow better than being at that wedding.

The agitated young man meanwhile was walking around his truck surveying the damage and attempting to call for help on his cell phone. Fortunately the only visible damage was a deep gouge in the chrome grill and continued down both front fenders all compliments of the rusty barbed wire fence now resting on the ground. Unable to get service on his cell phone he momentarily took his mind off the fresh battle scars on the rig and thought out loud,

"What else can go wrong today?"

"Anybody get hurt here?" Tom Jackson calmly asked the visitors in his pasture.

Neither Kevin nor Shari had seen or heard the horse and rider arrive upon the scene. Both of them had been lost in their own thoughts. Shari was embarrassed but now somehow relieved to have this man here.

"Hi Mr. Jacks ... Tom! You are not even going to believe what happened to us," she volunteered.

"It really does not matter how you arrived at this predicament but rather how we can remedy our situation," Tom responded.

"What do you mean ... our situation? We are the ones with the truck that is stuck in this damn pasture!" Kevin yelled as Tom climbed off Ginny and walked over to Kevin.

"First of all son, you just made an unwanted gate into my pasture which means the cattle can get out and onto the highway. We do not have free range around here anymore so you and I are going to fix 'my' fence." Tom ordered.

"Secondly son, do not ever swear in front of a lady with or without me in hearing proximity of you!"

"I am not your son and you cannot tell me ..." Kevin's challenge was never delivered.

Tom Jackson had just about enough of this kid. What happened next even surprised him. His left arm shot forward which allowed him to grab Kevin by the shirt collar and spin him sideways. At the same time Tom's free hand clutched Kevin's right wrist jerking it upwards between his shoulder blades. When it seemed as if Kevin's arm could go no further, Tom eased it up two inches higher. Kevin arched his back in sheer pain. Tom's left hand now held the back of Kevin's neck as he pushed Kevin's head into the driver door of his own truck. All one hundred and seventy eight pounds of this cowboy pinned the young man firmly without any chance of escape. Kevin's attempts to break free only brought his face flatter against the glass. He was not sure what hurt more, his nose and left cheekbone or his stubborn pride. Either way it appeared that Kevin should probably pay close attention to this man.

Tom spoke very slowly while keeping Kevin against the truck.

"Now, Mr. Kevin R. Daley, you seem to have a bit of rudeness in you which is not your most desirable trait that folks wish to enjoy. I personally think that you are probably a decent person but just have some difficulty conveying that quality. So, starting today, you are going to practice on it. When I let you go, you will apologize to both of the ladies, Shari Lynne Marie and my mare Ginny, for swearing in front of them. Then you will allow me the opportunity to teach you the craft of fixing a broken fence. Now, how does all this sound to you?" Tom asked.

The proximity of the glass against Kevin's lips would not allow him to verbalize his answer so his slight head nod was the only method for his affirmative response. Tom relaxed his hold on Kevin and walked towards Shari who was now standing and valiantly attempting to conceal a large smile. He removed his hat as he spoke.

"Shari, if you could find us a couple of small branches about six feet long it would help Kevin and me in our repair job. Thank you so much."

Tom turned to Kevin who was now standing quietly behind him. Tom put out his hand.

"I never had a chance to shake your hand back at Harley's. Please call me Tom."

Kevin returned the handshake while attempting to rub some feeling back into his face. His apology to the ladies was rather faint but satisfactory. He was still trying to understand how a man at least forty pounds lighter and probably twice his age threw him like that. Whatever the reason was, it gave Kevin a new respect for Tom Jackson. The two men proceeded to follow the deep tire tracks back to the new opening in the fence. Tom explained to Kevin that as soon as they fixed the fence they would get the truck back on all four wheels.

43

Confident that Tom had everything under control, Ginny sounded her approval with a familiar whinny. She casually lowered her head and returned to enjoying the green grass at her feet.

The repair job went smoothly for the new work team. Tom demonstrated to Kevin how the two branches would act as wooden links in order to mend the gaps in the barbwire fence. He explained that since it was impossible to reconnect the wire at its breaking points one must attach a broken strand to an end of the wood thus creating continuity in the line. This required two people since the wire was unable to stretch and it was necessary to maintain the original height of the fence. One person would hold the branch while the other does his best at nailing the broken end of barbwire to the wood. If the wire happens to sag at the repair point then you just use a third branch to act as a floating fence post for support. It was crude but an effective method of keeping the cattle on the inside of the enclosure. Not only was Kevin impressed with the whole procedure but also at Tom's wisdom in keeping an extra pair of leather gloves in his saddle bags. The barbwire was difficult to work with even if his hands did have the necessary added protection. Kevin's admiration for Tom Jackson was slowly increasing.

Tom stepped back and admired their completed work and also encouraged Kevin to do the same. He justified this action with the explanation that no job can be complete without it and it added that finishing touch. He was not sure why but Tom Jackson's own father had instilled this into him and he was now passing it on to Kevin. Shari applauded the two men and their accomplishment and let out a loud whistle that even made Ginny look in her direction. The trio walked back to Ginny's grazing spot and Tom once again returned his tools to the saddlebag.

"Keep those gloves on Kevin because now we will concentrate on getting your truck to a more drivable position," Tom advised.

As Tom unfastened the rope on the right side of his saddle he instructed Kevin to gather some large rocks and place them under the rear tires of his truck. This would allow the truck to gain traction as Ginny would assist by pulling in the same direction. Tom convinced Kevin that while he was searching for the correct size of rocks that he would go over the game plan with his horse to ensure a smooth operation. Tom turned his face to Ginny's ear and proceeded to whisper the instructions as Kevin started his search of the pasture.

Twenty minutes later Kevin placed the last rock behind the left rear tire of his truck. He then walked back to his new mentor as Tom was concluding his verbal instructions to Ginny,

"Now, you understand all of that girl?"

Kevin wondered what Tom could have been saying to his horse the whole time that he was collecting the rocks. Shari could not contain herself anymore and burst out in laughter as Tom joined in with her. Kevin still had a confused look on his face.

"Kevin R. Daley, you are a true city boy, aren't you?" She quizzed. "Don't you know when you have been conned by a cowboy?"

"What do you say that tomorrow we send him to the hardware store so that he can buy some board stretchers?" Tom bellowed.

"I still do not get it. I did just as Tom said. I placed the rocks under the tires while he made sure that Ginny understood what she is supposed to do," Kevin defended himself.

"Kevin, listen to me," Shari instructed. "Ginny is a ranch horse. She knows what to do when Tom is on top of her, not when he is talking to her. The only reason that Tom pretended to be talking to his horse was in order to let you collect all those rocks by yourself!"

"I am sorry Kevin, but I bet that you will never fall for that one ever again," Tom smirked.

Kevin knew better than to become angry so he just shook his head and smiled.

"I am afraid to ask you what I am supposed to do next." Kevin volunteered.

"All three of us will take part in this," Tom informed them. "After I tie the rope to Ginny and your bumper hitch, then you are going to get inside and start the engine. You will then have both of your feet holding the brake pedal as you put it into reverse. I will back Ginny up which will keep tension on our rope. When Shari relays my signal you will let the truck idle back down those rocks while letting your feet off of the brake. If, and I mean if, you must touch that gas pedal then you pretend that there is a raw quail egg on it. I do not want you to run over my horse especially with me on her. I am sure that I will someday die with my boots on but not with a truck running over me in reverse."

The three people accomplished the task without a flaw. Tom coiled the rope and fastened it securely to the saddle. Kevin and Shari retrieved their luggage and threw it into the bed of the pickup truck. Both of them watched as Tom walked Ginny over to the truck, dropped her reins to the ground and then opened the tailgate. He quickly removed her saddle and blanket and set them in near their luggage. The bridle and halter followed next. Tom placed his hand on Ginny's mane and proceeded all the way to her rump where he then gave her a sound slap.

"Ya ... ya ... g'yon! Get on home girl! We will be there soon," Tom whooped.

Ginny trotted a few yards away and then ran a circle around the truck and stopped abruptly. She lunged forward throwing her head to the ground and arched her back. Ginny bucked three times high into the air with all the vigor of a two-year-old filly. She quickly set her course for the ranch house and galloped away at full speed with her tail in the air.

Tom Jackson turned to face the bewildered couple staring back at him.

"You both have had a tough day and you are going to be my guests tonight. You really do not have much choice since my horse seems to have run off on me," Tom jested.

As the three new friends climbed in to the red 4x4 pickup truck, Tom continued speaking.

"I want all of us to go on a ride tomorrow. There is a place on my ranch that I think you should see. It is called Stump Rope and it might help you understand what has happened today."

The cab of the pickup truck was all but silent except for Tom Jackson's brief driving instructions and an occasional historical fact about certain landmarks that were still visible. The sun had nearly hidden itself from view behind the foothills that were directly in front of them. Tom had promised his guests that it would only be a few miles when the red 4x4 pickup truck had turned left off Highway 29 but he had failed to explain the difference between city and country miles to his traveling companions. It was the same as the American standard measuring unit and that metric system to Tom's way of thinking. A person will depart at point 'A' and will eventually arrive at point 'B' regardless of the type of vehicle or the speed that one travels. Sooner or later you will get to your destination.

Kevin had finally quit protesting mentally to his new cowboy friend on the other side of his truck. He knew he had his usual million-and-one things to do tomorrow before returning to work on Monday but now he had no choice, it would just have to wait. This was something that Kevin was not accustomed to doing but deep down inside there was a small feeling of relief. Maybe this is what everyone, especially Shari, had been trying to make him understand about his life. A person needs to take some time off now and then and just learn how to relax. Well, relax or not, Kevin still had to be able to see where he was driving so he blasted the windshield with a lengthy spray of water as the wiper blades cut through the layers of bugs. This action presented him with a whole new view of Dry Springs Road as he glanced over to receive Tom's approval on the procedure. The simple nod and wink said it all to Kevin, it was a job well done.

Shari felt her head snap backwards again as she fought the urge to fall asleep. The radio station was playing vintage country and western music that made her think about the barn dances that she would attend with her grandparents on Saturday nights. She remembered being a little girl and standing in her socks on her grandpa's shiny boots as he two stepped her around the crowded dance floor. She could still hear him counting out the beat as she would look up to see him smiling down at her. The smell of his after shave was still on her mind as she floated off to sleep. She felt her heavy head fall to the right and rest against Tom Jackson's shoulder as he carefully raised it in order to give her a softer pillow. She attempted to apologize to him but she was just too comfortable and the sleep felt very good. The last thing that she remembered hearing was someone saying good night young lady. Thank you she thought back in reply.

The cattle guard vibrated the pickup truck as it drove under the sign announcing the Flying 'B' Ranch. The first sight that the headlights caught was a black and white border collie sitting in the long driveway and directly behind her stood Ginny. The animals remained motionless even as the driver flashed the high beams at them.

The horse lowered her nose and met the dog's nostrils as they both sniffed at each other. The dog suddenly jumped backward remaining close to the ground with her rear and feathered tail protruding into the air. Her head was almost resting on the ground when she barked twice and remained in that position until Ginny pulled her head upwards and shook it defiantly. Then Ginny swiftly spun and trotted away from the truck with the dog running behind her and playfully jumping and nipping at her long tail. It was obvious that this was a ritual that they had practiced many times before this night.

A few seconds later a large barn and then a massive ranch house appeared in the lights. As they rolled past the barn Kevin was able to see Ginny now standing in her open stall and ahead was the Border collie patiently waiting at the front door of the ranch house.

"If you can keep your headlights on until I flip on the porch light then we will be able to see," Tom requested.

Shari was awakened by the sound of Tom's voice. She slowly sat upright in the seat as he climbed out of the truck. She shook her head and stretched her eyes open in the hopes that no one had noticed that she had been asleep for the last half hour. She and Kevin watched as Tom stopped a few steps from the house and brought his right hand up and gently tapped his chest. The Border collie responded by running to his side and sat looking up at him as her tail dusted the area behind her. Tom knelt down and stroked her behind the ears with both of his hands. She returned the affection by devouring his face thoroughly with tongue kisses and making certain that she did not miss a spot.

"Okay Bonnie, I missed you today also," Tom apologized.

He stood up and walked the remainder of the way to the house. Stopping, he opened the front door and reached inside. The porch light instantly illuminated the distance between the barn and the house. This allowed Kevin to turn off the headlights and truck engine. The only sound that could be heard was the pea gravel crunching under Tom Jackson's boots as he walked to the back of the pickup truck. Dropping the tailgate, Tom reached inside the bed and grabbed the two suitcases. He then walked back to the house and braced his back against the wooden screen door that Kevin was holding open for Shari. The door slammed closed behind Tom as he followed his guests through the enclosed porch and into the lighted kitchen. Tom shook his head as he passed the kitchen table where his lunch sack still sat and put the luggage down inside the living room.

Tom Jackson turned back to the kitchen, removed his hat, hung it on the wooden peg and walked over to the sink to wash his hands. He dried them with the faded dishtowel and looked at the young couple.

"Let's get you kids fed and then call it a night. The sun comes up really early in these parts and we have another long day ahead of us tomorrow," he told them.

All three of them agreed on the plan without even saying a word. Bonnie rested her head on her paws as she lay in front of the kitchen door. She was able to sleep now that everyone had returned home.

Shari was in her grandmother's kitchen helping prepare the morning meal for the branding crew. The men were talking loudly as the potent aroma of the brewing coffee hung in the air. It was a heavy smell that nearly covered her face as it touched her nostrils. She attempted to keep her eyes closed but the slam of the screen door chased the vivid memories away. She slowly opened her eyes but did not move her head. As she remained lying on her back, Shari carefully took in whatever she was allowed to see from this position. Kevin was still sleeping next to her with the pillow wrapped around his head in an attempt to expel the morning light coming in through the window. They were in a large bedroom decorated with items that a person would expect to find on a ranch. The adornments consisted of horseshoes, rusty spurs, an old rifle and of course looking back at her was that ever legendary 'Jackalope', the stuffed head of a jackrabbit with a set of antlers that would convince any city person that this unusual animal actually did exist in the wild. Shari had always wondered how much alcohol had been consumed by the first taxidermist who came up with the idea for this whimsical souvenir creature.

The young lady with the three first names finally gave in and crawled out of the comfortable bed. Shari was now on a personal quest to follow her nose and find that fresh coffee. She retraced her path from the previous night and found the kitchen with a note on the table. It was from Tom and did not need his name on it because it was directly to the point.

'I am doing some chores, so go ahead and help yourselves to anything you need'.

Next to the brief instructions was a plate of biscuits that even Shari's grandmother would envy. They had been made in this kitchen and not from a store bought cardboard tube as her grandfather would brag. Shari glanced at the clock on the wall with the silhouette of a bronc rider. He was holding on with one hand while the other was high in the air as the horse with its head held down arched its back and seemed to form the upside down letter 'U'. She could not remember the last time she had slept this late. She justified her long slumber with a large biscuit and a cup of coffee and then ventured back into the living room to view the collection of pictures on the wall.

The first thing that Shari noticed was that nearly all of the pictures were in black and white and went back many years. They consisted of family life and normal events on a working ranch. There were pictures of brandings, cowboys herding cattle, a man in a leather apron shaping a horseshoe with a hammer on an anvil and a young man sitting on a buckskin horse holding a small boy in front of him. The handsome young man was Tom Jackson. The next photograph was the same boy sitting on the horse with Tom standing on the ground and holding a very beautiful lady next to him. The faded inscription simply read, The Young Jackson Family. It was obvious that Tom and the lady were very much in love.

Kevin quietly walked up behind Shari and put his arms around her waist and gave her a kiss on the cheek. She nearly choked on her mouthful of biscuit as the hot coffee splashed out of her cup and hit Kevin's bare foot. He instantly jumped backward nearly falling into the leather recliner chair.

"Damn ... I mean darn!! That coffee is hot!" He yelled while looking over his shoulder to make sure that Tom was not within hearing range of his expletive that had slipped out.

"Well, you about scared me to death. That is what you get for sneaking up on me like that." She countered back at him.

Kevin proceeded to sit in the chair while rubbing his wounded foot.

"What are you doing?" He asked Shari.

"I was trying to look at some of these pictures before you gave me some new grey hairs. Not to add my insult to your injury but I just realized why Tom was able to throw you around so easily yesterday," she said while tapping the glass on one of the photos. "He was a mugger."

"What? You mean he robbed people?" Kevin was perplexed.

"You really need to get out more city boy," Shari laughed.

She proceeded to explain that Tom Jackson had competed in a rodeo event that is called wild horse racing and from the collection of dusty trophies on the mantle he must have been quite good at it. He was part of a three man team and it was his job to hold the wild horse behind the head in a bear hug while another team member would attempt to put the saddle on it. The horse, in the meantime, is not being the least bit cooperative and might have to be thrown to the ground by the mugger, which in this case was Tom Jackson. Once saddled, the horse would then be ridden a specified distance to cross the finish line in a certain time allowed. Kevin went from nursing his injured foot to touching the phantom pain in his left cheek.

"How did you kids sleep last night?" Tom startled them.

"Great!" They both answered.

"I just love looking at all of these pictures. Do you have any more of your wife and son?" Shari requested.

Tom quickly looked down at the floor and then gazed out the window at the three horses tied by the side of the barn. Shari knew instantly that the question made him very uncomfortable. There was a length of silence before Tom responded.

"They both left me a long time ago," Tom said with an empty tone in his voice.

Tom Jackson changed the subject by looking at Kevin.

"Kevin, I hope you won't mind riding bareback today. All of my boy saddles are in town for their annual polishing and I will not get them back until next week. I can lend you a pair of my boots for the ride. I think we are about the same size." Tom stated while attempting to maintain his poker face.

Kevin was afraid to ask the difference between a girl and a boy saddle. He was more concerned with how much longer before he let Tom know that he was not an experienced rider which was now compounded by his fear of riding without a saddle.

"Do you have your saddles down at the store that sells those board stretchers?" Shari inquired as seriously as possible.

Kevin's protests were muffled by Tom's and Shari's combined laughter.

"You two are hilarious. Let's all mess with the city boy, huh?" Kevin cackled trying to mimic the other two people.

"Naw, I have plenty of saddles for all genders and you are going to be riding Ginny today. I kind of figured that you could use a gentle horse. She will be the best one for you," Tom explained. "You always match a rider's experience level with the name of the horse."

Tom expounded more on the subject in order to help put Kevin more at ease.

"It is quite simple. You would never put a novice rider on an animal called Lucifer, Widow Maker, Death Wish or Lightning. The same way an old, bow-legged cowboy like me would never be caught on a horse named Slowpoke, Clover, Molasses or Glue Pot. You can think about it while we all have breakfast."

"Then how did Ginny get her name Tom?" Shari asked as she and Kevin sat down at the table.

"That is a story that I will share with you two on our ride to Stump Rope. Right now you are going to dine on a delicacy known in these parts as Tom Jackson's Coronary Express. So you kids start eating," Tom ordered as he piled their plates with the food.

Kevin and Shari dove in without waiting for a second invitation. Tom Jackson washed his hands at the sink and then joined his houseguests. He wondered how Kevin would react when he learned the truth about his own father and the place called Stump Rope.

The cottontail rabbit lifted its head from the meadow grass as it watched the trio of riders with the black and white dog leading them. They paid little attention to him so he felt safe continuing the morning meal as the man talked. Tom Jackson was telling the story of how Ginny earned her name.

Many years ago, when Ginny was a young filly, there was a hired hand by the name of Julius Kincade working on the ranch. He was in his twenties and quite popular with the ladies. He went by the nickname of 'Ace' due to his fondness and skill at the game of poker. It seems that Ace had decided to go to town one night and there he discovered his special lady with a wrangler from another ranch. It was evident that this had been going on for some time and it broke Julius 'Ace' Kincade's heart. Well, he decided to ride back to the Flying B Ranch and drown his sorrow in a bottle of gin. He accomplished the task all too well because when he stumbled back to the bunkhouse he forgot and left his half-filled bottle on the ground leaning against the corral.

The next morning as Tom Jackson was walking to the barn he noticed Ginny sticking her head through the fence and nimbly picking up the bottle with her mouth. She then proceeded to hold the neck of the open bottle in her lips and tip her head back as she consumed the remaining portion of the gin. She gently dropped the empty bottle over the corral and then did her best impersonation of a five and dime mechanical bucking horse. The whole time Tom swears she was smiling. So, from that moment on she has been known as Ginny. Tom let out a big laugh as he finished his story.

"Do you drink Tom?" Kevin inquired innocently.

"No, not anymore, not since the ... not since my wife and son left me," he answered without turning towards Kevin or Shari.

Shari could hear the remorse in Tom's response. She wished Kevin had not even asked such a personal question. Tom continued speaking as he looked forward.

"I am not against a man having a drink now and then as long as it does not make him stupid or mean," he told them. "When my family left me back then, that is exactly what I did for a good month. I got stupid and mean with a lip lock on my bottle. It was my best friend Harley White who came to my rescue and saved me. He still keeps that last bottle under his counter just as a reminder for me," Tom lamented. "That is why he is still my best friend."

"Where are my manners? I am going on all about myself. Let's hear about you kids!" Tom implored the other two riders.

Shari Lynne Marie jumped at the opportunity to change the subject. She was a city girl with a country heart. She grew up in Seattle but every summer, until she went off to college, she would stay at her grandparents' ranch in Arizona. It was a good balance with the best from both worlds. The big city gave her all the conveniences and an exposure to culture while the ranch life taught her how to be independent and able to think on her own. After she graduated college with a degree in political science she did a complete turn and entered the world of fashion and was now the buyer for a national chain of boutique stores. That is how she and Kevin met in St. Louis. She was opening a new store and he was attending a computer conference. The rest was like the fairy tale story ... 'and they lived happily ever after'. She concluded the account looking directly at Tom with crossed eyes and bouncing her head from side to side.

Kevin R. Daley went next after a little hesitation. He was very brief about his childhood other than he had never known his real father. His mother always worked to make ends meet and spent any free time with her son. He grew up as a loner with very few friends but had a passion for electronics. This led him into the computer world, which eventually evolved into a lucrative manufacturing company of his own. His computer distribution was international. Kevin had invested his earnings wisely and now he and his mother were financially comfortable. He quickly pointed to the fact that if it had not been for his cousin's wedding yesterday then he and Shari would never have met Tom Jackson.

Tom Jackson eased his horse to a stop. His fellow riders did the same. Tom removed his hat and wiped his brow with his shirtsleeve. He returned the hat to his head and looked at the young couple. His focus was directly on Kevin. Tom waited a few seconds and then drew a long breath.

"Kevin, in a manner of speaking, you and I have met before. You were too young to even remember it. You were only about six months old then. It was the last time that I ever saw you and your mother." Tom carefully chose his next words. "It was at your daddy's funeral!"

The silence hung in the air as Shari watched the reaction on Kevin's face. She shifted her weight in the saddle.

"Then you do know my mother, don't you?" Kevin begged.

"Yes, I knew your mother many years ago and it was your daddy who took my wife and son from me!" Tom finally said.

The look on Kevin's face was total confusion. He listened to Tom Jackson's words but did not comprehend anything that the man was saying.

"Let's walk the horses the rest of the way. We are just a short distance from Stump Rope and it is time that I did some explaining," Tom admitted.

The three people led their horses in silence. The only sound that could be heard was Bonnie's barking as she playfully chased the cottontail rabbit.

The waterfall ran down the smooth rock face and collected into a deep pool below. The water continued to spill into a creek that wound through the tall trees and moved in the direction towards the ranch house and barn. The moist air greeted the trio as they made their way through the clearing surrounded by waist high ferns and tied their horses to the fallen Elm tree. This setting was beyond the word beautiful. It had the feeling of a peacefulness that touched a person deeply inside their soul. The three friends were at Stump Rope.

Shari silently walked over to Tom Jackson and stood in front of him without saying a word. She knew how much this place called Stump Rope meant to him as she looked deeply into his eyes. There was a reflection of happiness in them as Tom grinned back at her. Shari Lynne Marie wrapped her arms around Tom and engulfed him with a tight hug as he did the same to her.

"Thank you Tom, thank you very much!" Shari whispered to him.

Tom Jackson did not have to say a word. Shari knew that he was very glad to have them both at his special place called Stump Rope.

"Hey you two, I cannot leave you alone for a second!" Kevin joked as he walked back towards them.

"What a wonderful place this is!" Shari exclaimed as she moved backward two steps and then turned a full circle taking in the entire view.

"Yeah, now you kids can see what I have been talking about," Tom boasted as he walked back to his horse and untied a couple of blanket rolls behind the saddle.

He walked to the most level spot of ground and spread the fabric out and then went to Shari's horse to retrieve a small picnic bag.

"Kevin, if you would," Tom instructed him, "Go down to the edge of the creek and you will find a rope wrapped around that Spruce tree. The other end is attached to a net in the water and it is filled with cold sodas and beer. Bring it back up here so that we can have some drinks with our lunch."

Kevin accomplished the task quickly realizing how thirsty he was and certain that the other two felt the same as he did. He was also amazed at Tom Jackson's simple ingenuity out here in the middle of nowhere. He set the dripping treasure next to one of the blankets and wiped his hands on the back of his jeans.

"I thought that you did not drink Tom?" Kevin quizzed his host.

"That is true but it does not mean that my guests cannot have a cold beer after a long ride. Just help yourself to whatever looks good," Tom answered.

The lunch and cold drinks came at a perfect time of the day. The horses needed a rest and the city kids realized that their tail ends could use a break from the saddles. Even Shari had forgotten just how hard that leather could be on her bottom side. She felt especially sorry for Kevin. Having watched him ride made her think of a comment repeated many times by her grandfather, 'the only difference between you and a sack of spuds in that saddle is that at the end of the day we can eat the potatoes'. She quickly brought the can of beer to her mouth to conceal the smile on her face.

"Did you kids get enough to eat?" Tom asked looking at the empty plates in front of Kevin and Shari.

They were both in agreement on the answer. Neither person could find room for another bite, the cherry pie would just have to wait until later in the day.

"What do you say that we take a little walk and make some room for that dessert?" Tom coaxed. "There is something that I would like you two to share with me."

Kevin and Shari eased themselves up from the ground and followed Tom down a faintly visible foot path that led through a group of saplings about two hundred feet from their picnic spot. They looked at each other somewhat confused as they continued to follow Tom past the trees and into another clearing. At the entrance Tom stopped and gestured with his arm for them to go first. Kevin and Shari obliged him as he followed behind them. What met them on the other side stopped the couple in their tracks.

A white picket fence confined an area about twenty by twenty feet. The outside perimeter was surrounded entirely by various wild flowers. The only break in the flowers was the hinged gate that allowed entry into the enclosure. Directly in the center of all this was an old stump deeply rooted in the ground and on each side of it was a headstone. Shari knew at once why Tom Jackson had only old photographs of his wife and son in his home. His family was here, buried at Stump Rope.

Kevin and Shari quietly walked to the edge of the gate and respectfully read the inscriptions on the markers. They stopped at the dates of death realizing that both mother and son had died on the same day. What was even more unusual was that it was a date that Kevin knew all too well.

"Kevin, they died on your ....!"

Tom interrupted Shari before she could finish.

"That is right Kevin, my family died on the same day that you were born. That is the day that your daddy took my family from me!" Tom confessed.

"None of this makes any sense to me. What are you saying?" Kevin pleaded.

"You kids go back to the picnic area and I will be there shortly. I need to spend a few minutes with my family now. All of this will make sense when I explain the whole story. Please, trust me," Tom assured them.

Kevin was holding Shari's hand as they began their walk back to the blankets. They turned to look at the graves where Tom knelt in silence. Bonnie was by his side as she lay at the foot of the stump with her head resting on her paws. She would stay with Tom until he was ready to leave.

Bonnie was first to join Kevin and Shari at the blanket as they sat and shared small talk. The Border collie obediently laid at the edge of the blanket within an arms-reach of Shari who immediately began running her hand down the dog's neck. Bonnie took full advantage of Shari's talents by rolling onto her back and exposing her soft belly to this young lady's touch. The stomach scratching was so good that Bonnie moved her legs in a manner of someone riding an imaginary bicycle. Bonnie's glazed eyes were fixed on Shari as the collie let out a deep doggy moan.

Tom Jackson walked up to the amusing canine spectacle as he balanced three pieces of cherry pie on paper plates. The metal forks and napkins protruded from his shirt pocket. He set the desserts down in front of Kevin and placed the napkin wrapped utensils next to them.

"Why don't we all get some of this great cherry pie baked by Mrs. Bowlen. It will make you smile like a wife on her husband's payday," Tom laughed.

The three of them all smiled as they enjoyed the dessert while Tom told the story of the Bowlen brothers' big shootout in the alley on the previous day. He also talked about his own brother and how close they had been and that he would have been old enough to start collecting his social security payments next year. Shari remembered seeing pictures on the living room wall of a youthful Tom Jackson standing next to a young man in a military uniform. This man and Tom were beaming and saluting at each other as the picture was taken. Shari thought it was best not to ask Tom about his brother.

"Do you kids believe in fate?" Tom caught the young couple off guard with the question that seemed to come out of nowhere.

Tom Jackson did not give the pair a chance to answer him. He expounded on the subject as they listened. He clarified that things in this great world happen for a purpose. A person or people are in a certain place at a certain time for a certain reason. That is what happened to all of them yesterday. Their paths crossed not just once, not twice but three different times in the course of the same day. It was fate.

"It was destiny that we were all supposed to meet yesterday. It's just as simple as that!" Tom continued, "now let me tell you about my family, Stump Rope and what happened twenty seven years ago next month on the day that Kevin R. Daley Jr. was born."

Tom Jackson lowered his head and closed his eyes as if he was in prayer. He gently kneaded his forehead with his left hand and slowly inhaled a large breath through his nostrils. He held it for a few seconds and then exhaled out of his mouth. Joining his hands together in his lap, Tom deliberately raised his head and reopened his eyes. Looking past Kevin and Shari, Tom Jackson began to tell his story.

The Flying B Ranch had been in Tom Jackson's family for generations and ranching was all he had ever known. Tom was now the last of the Jacksons. His brother had never had the chance to have any children and Tom's only son was buried next to his wife. It would all end with Tom when it came time for him to leave this world.

Tom Jackson had married his high school sweetheart two years after they graduated. Her name was Kelley O'Brien and she was the perfect example of beauty and courage in an Irish lady. The day of their wedding her father told Tom Jackson the 'two nevers' of a happy marriage. Never love her less than you did the day before and never let her forget that you are the luckiest son of a bitch in the world. Tom Jackson had never forgotten those words and the promise that he made to Mr. O'Brien.

Tom Jackson Junior was born six years later to the proudest parents in the county. Harley White was the first person to thank Kelley for giving Tom Junior her looks. Harley was worse than the grandparents when it came to spoiling the boy. Tom Junior always referred to Harley White as Uncle Harley.

The young family spent any free time here at Stump Rope. It was Tom Junior that initiated the name of this spot by practicing his roping for that special day that he would get to go with his father. The stump that now divides the two graves is the same stump that he always used for practicing his rope throws. As soon as Tom Junior was five years old he would be allowed to go with his father and help round up wild horses.

Eventually that inevitable day arrived. Tom remembered his son insisting on a handshake rather than a hug before he climbed into the pickup truck for the ride to town. Tom Junior was a man now since the next day he was going with his father to bring back wild horses. Tom Jackson respected his son's request. He instead gave his wife the hug and reminded her that he was the luckiest son of a 'gun' in the world and to drive carefully. She kissed him and also thanked him for altering her father's saying in front of their son. That was the last time Tom Jackson ever saw his family alive.

That same morning another young couple was at the county hospital awaiting the birth of their first child. They were Kevin and

Angela Daley, the soon to be parents of Kevin R. Daley Jr. After their new son arrived in this world and that he knew his wife and son were doing well, Kevin Daley headed back home to take care of the work on his ranch. He promised his wife that he would return to the hospital that evening. Kevin Daley made the mistake of stopping at the Water 'N Hole Saloon out on Highway 29 so that he could have a beer and celebrate the birth of his new son. Unfortunately, his good intentions turned into an afternoon of drinking with his buddies. Determined that he was able to drive, he left the bar and made it about ten miles down the road where he came around a curve too fast and collided with a pickup truck killing both the driver and passenger. The occupants of that vehicle were Kelley and Tom Jackson Junior. Kevin Daley did live up to the promise that he had made to his wife. He did get back to the hospital that evening but it was by way of an ambulance.

    Kevin Daley recovered from the accident and then stood trial for two counts of manslaughter. He was convicted and sentenced to fifteen years in prison. Tom Jackson attended the trial each day and it was the first time in his life that he ever felt hatred for another human being. Kevin Daley never made it to his first parole hearing. Six months after entering prison he died when a laundry boiler that he was repairing exploded. Tom Jackson surprised the small community when he attended Kevin Daley's funeral. He knew the pain that Angela Daley felt with the loss of her husband. Tom extended his sympathies to the new mother and her infant son. That was the last time that Tom Jackson saw Angela and Kevin R. Daley Jr.

EPILOGUE

The red tailed hawk rode the warm thermals as it watched the red 4x4 pickup truck slowly turn left onto Highway 29 North. The young couple inside were laughing and making plans for a trip. It did not matter where as long as they took enough time off to relax and enjoy each other.

The cowboy stepped back into his house and hung the weathered hat on a wooden peg in the kitchen. He walked over to his desk in the living room and sat down. He wiped his hand on his thigh as he thought for a few moments. He picked up the phone and punched in the number for his attorney. It was about time to finally make a decision on the Flying B Ranch.

CPSIA information can be obtained
at www.ICGtesting.com
Printed in the USA
BVHW042328160422
634374BV00006B/177